DEDICATION

To the Church of Christ in the Ottawa Valley that taught
me to walk in the peace of Christ. I will always be in
gratitude to Pastor Mark Redner and his father Jim Redner
for being patient with me during my early days of
salvation. They are great friends and patient men of God.

CONTENTS

ACKNOWLEDGMENTS

Thank-you to Jeeva Sam for starting Destiny Word of the Day. Without his encouragement to write for that blog this book would not have come about.

Thanks to my mother for the early lessons on learning to be healed on the inside.

Thanks to Mark and Kiwanda Redner for being patient as I learned to walk in Christ.

Thanks to Jim Redner for walking me through the path of healing.

Thanks to Pastor Joe Moniz for being there for me during some difficult hours.

And thanks to my precious wife, Lydia, who is the greatest example of a person filled with peace that I know.

1 PEACE FOR THE CHRISTIAN LIFE

The Christian Life is not always an easy life. Each day we are made new. Many times we are shocked by the behavior of others who call themselves Christians because they don't seem to be Christian at all, and yet, they are Christian, but then, I am also Christian even when my behavior lacks character and perfection. This is the Grace of God.

We have all fallen short of the glory of God in one way or another in our lives. The sin that rages in the earth is like a plague and there are times when I still feel overcome by it. But it is no longer I who lives, but Christ who lives within me. When I succumb to a failing he is faithful and makes me new. Even in the face of a crisis in my life I can be reborn to higher heights in God.

Recently I was struggling in my spirit. I felt pain as a result of the change that was taking place in my life. I was feeling left behind and overwhelmed, and so I asked my wife to pray for me for peace in my heart. We were driving home from church at the time.

As she was praying a giant golden eagle took to flight right beside our van. I was awed by the encounter. I had never seen such a giant eagle before. It was majestic and bigger than I ever imagined. Hope rose in my heart as I felt the Holy Spirit was refreshing my heart.

1

Isaiah 40:31 comes to mind from this experience: *"But those who hope in the LORD will renew their strength. They will soar on wings like eagles; they will run and not grow weary, they will walk and not be faint."*

I knew that the lord was saying that my strength would be renewed and that things would turn around.

Most of us have gone through very difficult circumstances. We have failed in one way or another. Perhaps you have failed in so many ways that you don't know whether God can accept you any longer. The truth is that he loves you very much.

David failed when he had an adulterous relationship with Bathsheba. Not only did he commit adultery, but he later had her husband killed when he got her pregnant. He married her immediately after. When he was confronted by his behavior he repented and turned back toward God.

It is said of David that he was a man after God's own heart. I want to be a man like that too. Do you?

Repentance and purity are key! If we don't love perfectly then we must repent when we have hurt those around us. We must seek restoration and right relationship with everyone. We might even have to restore what we have stolen from others.

We do this because we want to have a pure heart before God. We want to stay in the place of his voice where we can hear the sweet harmony of his spirit. I don't want to walk away from his voice and so I am willing to lay down my pride in order to get to that place. Repentance and forgiveness are difficult to offer sometimes but they are keys to purity in Christ.

If the Lord says jump we jump and if he says stay then we stay. Whatever he says goes and that is how you are blessed in this life.

I pray for you today. I ask the Lord to touch your brokenness and to bring healing to the most difficult places in your heart. I ask the Lord to pour out his oil and wine over your spirit so that you might rise like the eagle into the atmosphere of the Holy Spirit.

2 PEACE FOR THE INNER MAN

Ephesians 3:14-19

For this reason I bow my knees before the Father, from whom every family in heaven and on earth is named, that according to the riches of his glory he may grant you to be strengthened with power through his Spirit in your inner being, so that Christ may dwell in your hearts through faith—that you, being rooted and grounded in love, may have strength to comprehend with all the saints what is the breadth and length and height and depth, and to know the love of Christ that surpasses knowledge, that you may be filled with all the fullness of God.

When you enter into the realm of God's love it is about His strength of feeling in your inner man. He is inside of you like a strong breath pulsating in your heart and in your being.

His presence becomes a guiding force. When you feel it you feel capable of doing anything. Ideas will come into your mind that would seem bizarre except for the fact that you are drunk on His Holy presence. God in your inner man will cause you to walk on water. You will jump and fly into mid air. Nothing seems impossible when God is closer to you than the breath you breathe.

I keep praying more and more to know the love of God. I want to experience that love. I want to be transformed by it. I don't want anything to come between me and my God and I am willing to do whatever He says to remain in the place of His presence. When God speaks I am quick to listen because His spirit is all I desire.

The things of this world actually grow strange and dim when you encounter the glory of His presence. I remember being fond of the strangest things before Jesus but when He came into life my heart everything else paled in comparison to His wonderful presence. I was willing to give up everything to stay in that place of presence. I turned and walked away from the world in order to gain the one thing my soul longed for more than anything else and that was God.

And for these ten years I have been turning from the world more and more. In the end the only thing that will remain is love. The only thing that I will take with me into eternity is the presence of God. I love him more than life. I want Him to be more real to me tomorrow than He is even today.

He is pruning me and cleansing me and making me more into His image. Each time He speaks to me I become more like Him. He whispers change and I change.

I have learned to listen quickly because the rewards of His love and peace far outweigh anything that you or this world could give to me. I have been tempted in many ways but I continue in His presence because it is better than all other temptations.

It is by faith that I have stepped into this place. At one point I made the decision that Jesus was all I needed. I determined in my heart that all other things that I needed in this life were not as important as Him. I have not regretted one moment of my life in Christ. Before Christ my life was filled with regrets. I was filled with shame and sorrow. Now these no longer rule my life.

I am ruled by the peace of God. I am rooted and grounded in love. Even when I make mistakes He loves me. Even when I fail He is there. He makes a way where there seems to be no way. As long as I do what He says, and I am obedient then I remain in Him.

I pray for you and for me today that we will remain through every storm, through every crisis and through every trial. I pray that you will walk on water and that you will see the putrid parts of your heart turned into the finest wine.

3 PEACE AS WE SACRIFICE

1 Corinthians 1:18-21

For the word of the cross is folly to those who are perishing, but to us who are being saved it is the power of God. For it is written: "I will destroy the wisdom of the wise, and the discernment of the discerning I will thwart."

Where is the one who is wise? Where is the scribe? Where is the debater of this age? Has not God made foolish the wisdom of the world? For since, in the wisdom of God, the world did not know God through wisdom, it pleased God through the folly of what we preach to save those who believe.

Have you ever felt yourself fearing what the world thought of your faith? I will admit that when I was younger I used to worry about what philosophers and the media thought of my faith. I went as far as to renounce my faith at one point in my life because this fear was so strong.

The opinions of men are mortal in nature and have a certain lifespan that ends at the grave. Each one of us will appear before the Father one day and have to account for the opinions that we allowed to influence our lives. We will stand before Him and give account for our beliefs that were not aligned with His word. I can assure you that in that moment He will not say, "Oh that was a very good reason for not believing me."

We are to trust and obey Him. We are to renounce the thoughts and ways of the world even when they seem to have a speck of wisdom about them, and if we are easily swayed by these thoughts, then we probably shouldn't be listening to them at all.

Too much sugar might taste good, but in the end it will make you sick. It is the same with the thoughts of men. They seem to have an air of superiority about them, but in the end they cause emotional sickness and spiritual death.

We cannot take ourselves out of this world, but it doesn't mean that we have to watch every movie that comes out or watch every show or news program on TV. We don't have to read the latest blogs or newspapers. We can turn these things off. These actually can become clutter that will inhibit us from walking in greater faith.

When you feed on a thought pattern that is not of Christ more than the word of God, it is going to have an effect on your ability to believe the things that God says. In fact listening to the clutter can actually stop you from recognizing the voice of God when He does speak.

The Psalmist said, *"Oh, how I love your law! I meditate on it all day long"* (Psalm 119:97); and again *"Your word is a lamp for my feet, a light on my path"* (Psalm 119:105); and yet again, *"Your word have I hid in my heart, that I might not sin against you"* (Psalm 119:11).

It is when we cherish the word more than the world that our paths become straight. It is when we *trust in the Lord with all of our hearts and lean not on our own understandings, but acknowledge Him in all of our ways,* that our paths are strong and secure (Proverbs 2:5-6).

The life of a Christian is a life of sacrifice, but the sacrifice does not seem so costly when the benefits of the Kingdom begin to appear at your feet. I haven't sacrificed anything for God that He hasn't given back to me many times in this life, not to mention what awaits me in the life to come.

We need to start obeying Him and listening to Him more than we listen to the philosophers and sages of this world. I don't even subjugate myself to their thoughts anymore. I choose to believe the evidence that my faith is presented with in Christ. My well-being and peace of heart are evidence to me that I have made the right decision.

4 A BAPTISM OF LOVE AND PEACE

1 Corinthians 13:13

And now these three remain: faith, hope and love. But the greatest of these is love.

The greatest gift that God offers mankind is His unfailing love. When God's love penetrates your heart you are filled with an awe that is hard to put into words. There are times that His love becomes so powerful inside of me that I am left only to tears.

I would say that the greatest weapon that a man or woman of God could ever have is the love of God. When the love of God fills your heart people will come from as far away as the moon to look into your eyes. They want to see that pure fire of God inside of you because love is contagious.

The enemy hates the love of God because it can tear his Kingdom apart within moments. He will do whatever he can to stop that love from spreading because to him it is a virus that will destroy his purposes every time.

For you and I love becomes the safe place of the presence of God. It is the shelter that keeps us from the storm.

Recently I was flying across the United States when I

encountered a crazy storm over San Antonio. My friends who lived there told me that it was one of the worse thunder storms that they had seen in a long time. As I was flying through this weather pattern the plane that I was on started to jerk and shake. My stomach felt like it was inside my mouth. I sat there in joy because I knew the love of God in my heart.

There is nothing that can destroy a man who is surrounded by the love of God. No fear can overtake him. No weapon can destroy him. God's love is like a safe refuge from the greatest destructions that can come upon us. Certainly a plane can shake and fear can grip the heart of a mortal man, but I am no longer a mere mortal in Christ but I am now an eternal spirit, born anew in Christ who will live for all eternity. This body might be torn apart but my spirit shall live forevermore. I shall be like the stars in the sky. I shall shine with the righteousness of Christ forever and ever.

This love lives inside of me and those that come near me will be changed, not because of me but because of His love that lives within me. This is the power of God and is the greatest power.

I can prophesy accurately and often do. I can heal the sick and often do. I have seen crazy signs and wonders but it is this love that dwells in my heart that draws people to Christ.

The way to love is through the healing of the heart. We must let God touch our hearts and heal the brokenness inside of us. When fear grips me there is an ungodly root that God wants to pull out. The way is through forgiveness and repentance. When I repent of the evil that lurks deep within my heart then I make room for the love of God to burn even brighter.

When God highlights a need for healing within my heart I get excited because I know that I am going to have more of the love of Jesus inside of me. It is this love that I am addicted to the most, but please do not pray for deliverance for me from this addiction because it is the greatest medication that I have ever taken. When I remain in love I remain in peace and I can face every trial that comes.

I pray for you today and ask the Holy Spirit to change you from glory to glory that you may also be baptized in love.

5 THE EASY YOKE OF HEALING

Matthew 11:29
*Take my yoke upon you and learn from me, for I am
gentle and humble in heart, and you will find rest for
your souls.*

There have been times that I have felt the humility of
God in my life. It is like a fresh summer rain when it
comes upon me. I know this humility is not me but it
comes upon me like a gift so that I can feel the
gentleness of God.

You see there is no one like our God who is able to give
such purity and wonder to His people. He lifts the
heaviest burdens off of our shoulders like they are
nothing. Burdens that I have carried all my life roll away
when God speaks to them.

The yoke of the Lord is to carry out His will. When we
step into His will for our lives we come into a place of
great peace. Even when what God says seems
impossible, as I do it, a refreshing breeze enters into my
spirit.

There have been times that the Lord has had to be stern
with me and speak to me about my actions and
behavior. He will come and tell me to do certain things
which seem overwhelming, but as I step into them I
have found two things occur. First God makes a way

where there seems to be no way and secondly he heals my emotions so that I can handle the new assignment.

Before every new assignment God comes and reveals the negatives of my heart to me. Sometimes there are lies that I have been in agreement with, or there are areas where I need to repent or forgive. As I do these things He enables me to walk into a greater and more open space for my life.

Recently the Lord wanted to align me to some new people to help grow my ministry, but just before he did He showed me in a dream that I did not feel worthy to walk with these people. When I was young the enemy came to me and told me that I was a low class person who could never fit into the upper ranks or classes.

This lie had stopped me from getting promoted over and over in my life. I didn't realize that I believed this either, but when God revealed it to me in a dream I was quick to repent for coming into agreement with the lie and asked him to forgive me. The very next day two senior religious leaders approached me to do work with them.

What we need to understand is that there are many things that keep us from God's perfect plan for our lives. When we trust Him and do what He says, which from my experience is very easy, then the way is opened before us.

Often fear will keep us from the breakthrough. We may not trust God with our future. We may think he doesn't have good things in store for us, but I have come to understand that He is a good God and only has good for me. I now give Him permission to always correct me as soon as I need correction and I believe because of this I have advanced quickly in the Kingdom.

Moreover the new peace that rises upon me is reward enough for doing what he says.

I pray that you too will open your hearts to Christ for healing. I know as you do you will reach your destiny much quicker. Remember His yoke is easy and His burden is light.

6 PEACE LIKE A FIRE WITHIN ME

John 14.27
"Peace I leave with you; my peace I give you. I do not give to you as the world gives. Do not let your hearts be troubled and do not be afraid."

Your chains have no power to remain when Christ is your King because as a child of the King you have access to the greatest healing power that the world has ever known. Jesus has a way of entering deep into the greatest emotional wounds of your life and bringing peace where there is no peace. He remains calm when you are not calm. He sits in the back of your boat resting when your greatest storms do rise.

Jesus is the great physician. He is the master healer. He has gone to prepare a place for you in heaven where there is no more sorrow and no more pain. Even on this side of eternity we are afforded the luxury of great peace because *"God is our refuge and strength, an ever-present help in trouble." (Psalms 46:1)*

There is nowhere you can run from His presence. There is no situation that you are in that He cannot help you get out of. It doesn't matter what you have done He will forgive you. Even what we consider to be the greatest sins can be forgiven in Christ. God has a way of forgiving and healing the gravest sins – all through the blood of Jesus.

Before I knew the Lord I didn't think He could forgive me because I was a wicked sinner. There was nothing that I did not allow myself to do. But I will tell you this - that even when I was lost in sin and had no mind for God - He came to me and spoke to me. I wasn't even searching for Him. I was thinking about other things. I didn't even consider that He would forgive me and I didn't even realize that I needed forgiveness for my sin.

In that moment when He spoke to me great conviction fell on my soul because I knew the purity of the one who was speaking into my life. I knew the truth of my sinful nature but I didn't think He could forgive such a great sinner as I.

And yet He began to speak deep into my heart telling me of the plan that He had for my life and that He loved me very much. It was too much for me to hear and I told Him to stop speaking and yet He continued to speak into my life.

Through time I began to realize that the shame and guilt of my sin had no hold upon my life. I could feel His righteousness, joy and peace rising in me. I began to understand that I was bound by sin no longer and that my life was made new - all this through the voice of God speaking into my life.

Each day my mind is renewed and His love for me I feel strongly like a fire in my chest. He is the greatest thing that has ever happened to me.

When you understand that righteousness and good living is a gift from God then you can begin to pray this prayer in **Isaiah 45:8**, *"You heavens above, rain down* *my righteousness; let the clouds shower it down."* The blessing of the Lord is to bring righteousness into the repentant heart. Not by works of the flesh but by the grace of God. He has great things in store and all you have to say is "yes Lord."

Get ready for a visitation of righteousness. Get ready for the fire of God to burn in your heart. Get ready for God to come closer than He has ever been before. Your destiny is established so just ask Him for more.

7 PEACE IN THE MIDST OF TROUBLE

Psalm 46:1-3
God is our refuge and strength, a very present help in trouble. Therefore we will not fear though the earth gives way, though the mountains be moved into the heart of the sea, though its waters roar and foam, though the mountains tremble at its swelling.

Are you afraid? Are you easily shaken? This is a fair question. When troubles arise do you run and hide? Are you easily disturbed? Does anger enter your heart and frustration take over? Do your eyes look to your circumstances or to the power of God? Do you see God or do you see the giant?

David was a boy, but killed a giant man. He saw the circumstances that stood before him. He was not compelled by his people, family or even the king to enter into that battle. He could have chosen to walk away and no one would have questioned why. Certainly, they would not have even thought of him as a choice. He was a boy, after all. But something rose in his heart. He knew his God and he knew that this giant before him was no match for Him.

I get calls from people all the time asking me if they are going to be alright. They want to hear me say, "Yes everything is going to be ok...don't worry because God has your situation taken care of." They call me because they want the confidence that is in my heart to speak to their situations. They do not have that confidence on their own, so they are looking for a champion to command that darkness out of their lives.

If only they could be like David! If only they could see from God's perspective! If only faith would rise up in their hearts so that they would see their circumstances from heaven's eyes! They would not worry one more day. They would not lose their cool ever again.

It is actually not possible for you to experience anything but blessing in Christ. Trials will come, but from that trial will rise a fire in your heart to conquer lands. The devil may come at you one way, but he will run away in seven directions. Yes, the devil always tries, but he never succeeds.

One of my preacher friends called me two days ago. He was anxious because his dog attacked another dog causing so much damage that he was liable for $5000.00 (that he did not have) to pay the other owner's veterinarian expenses. He called me wanting me to get a word from the Lord for him. An excitement rose up in my heart, so I told him so. I told him I felt like an explosion of increase was about to take place in his life.

He told me that he had to put half the amount on his credit card and go to the bank for a loan for the other half. In the natural it didn't look good...but God!

The next day he called me back very relieved. He said that his house insurance covered the damages.

The enemy tries, but he cannot succeed. You have to know this in your heart that no matter what arises against you, the Lord has a way out. There is nothing going to conquer your life. Your enemy will not be able to shame you because you have the Almighty God as your best friend and He is looking out for you.

Have you read Psalm 18 and seen the response of God when His boy was surrounded by his enemies? God came down to earth riding on a cloud of glory and squashed those enemies beneath His feet.

His peace will rise upon you in trials that come. You will feel His presence in a way that you never imagined possible. Even in the most difficult trials God will be there with you. There is no one or nothing that can stop Him from coming to the aid of the one He loves.

So bury your head in His shoulder today and ask Him to come near to your heart. He gives good gifts to His children and there is no greater gift than His peace.

8 PEACE IN THE FACE OF GIANTS

James 1:2-4

Consider it pure joy, my brothers and sisters,"whenever you face trials of many kinds, 3 because you know that the testing of your faith produces perseverance. 4 Let perseverance finish its work so that you may be mature and complete, not lacking anything.

I love it when the Lord speaks to me and says "Darren everything is going to be alright." It is probably the greatest word of encouragement that He can give to me. He says this to me whenever I need to hear it, which – honestly – is almost every single day.

I am like you. Many things come into my life that stir worry and concern. I must continue in the word of God in order to assure myself that I am going to be alright. I have had financial problems. I have gone through messy situations on the job and in the church. I have had health issues. I have had family and friends attack me and I have watched as some of my family members have gone through outrageous trials of their own.

So to hear God say that everything is going to be alright means as much to me as it probably would to you.

What I have come to understand is the power of the cross. I do not apologize for hiding beneath it. My entire provision is in the place of Jesus' finished work there. My health, my income, and my well-being are all tied to what he did for me.

I am thankful that my God has grafted me into the vine of Christ. I am thankful that my complete salvation and deliverance is assured. I may stand on the banks of the Red Sea looking at the enemy approaching with mighty power from behind, but I know my God. The sea before me will open up and I shall cross over to the other side on dry ground. I shall only look with my eyes and see my enemy's plans for my life destroyed by the mighty hand of God.

I may stand before a giant that curses the very core of my belief in God, but I shall be empowered to throw a stone right between my enemy's eyes and watch as he comes crashing down before me.

A thousand false prophets may declare - for the entire world to hear - that the Christian God has no power, but I know that my God is real and that His power and His word will stand. It doesn't concern me that I might have to stand alone because I know that in the hour of my testing my God shall stand with me strengthening me like He strengthened Daniel in the Lion's Den, like He strengthened the three young men in the furnace of fire. He won't leave me in that place of suffering alone but He will come into the fire and bring me peace.

In order to understand that God will be with you in the fire you actually have to go through some fires. James said to consider it pure joy when you go through trials of many kinds because you know that the testing of your faith will produce perseverance. He said that when we persevere under trial our faith shall become mature and complete in Christ.

God's encouragement is what strengthens me to face the trials that I face. When he says everything is going to be alright this thought enters the core of my being and the truth of it is simply known in Christ.

I pray for you today. May God strengthen you in the face of all your trials. I pray that you will overcome the world even as Jesus has overcome and now sits by His father in heaven.

9 PEACE FOR MY BROKENNESS

Romans 12:2
Do not conform to the pattern of this world, but be transformed by the renewing of your mind. Then you will be able to test and approve what God's will is--his good, pleasing and perfect will.

The peeling back of the broken layers of the heart is a process I am not sure will ever end on this side of eternity, but it is a process we must submit ourselves to in order to become the perfect bride of Christ without spot or wrinkle.

The renewing of the mind is a substantial thing. It is not a momentary "bang" and it is finished and over. Jesus died on the cross for our sins once and for all but our minds are renewed out of the 'old man' and into the 'new man' on a day-to-day basis.

There are so many fears that bind a man's heart. He isn't even aware of many of them. These fears have a way of leading us into compromising situations where we surrender the best that God has to offer us for nothing good. Our fears have the power to trap us with the great part of humanity that is headed into darkness and death.

The darkness causes shadows to manifest within our heart and shadows have a way of looking bigger than they really are. Our shadows and fears not only bind us but also bind others that look to us for strength.

The sounds of fear that come from my own heart become the foundation of fear for generations to come. If I am not set free from fear then it is likely that my own family members will be bound by the same fears.

But Jesus came to set the captives free. He will set me free and he will set the generations to follow free as well. The captivity of my heart is greater than I first imagined. Even last night I was in the mansion of my mind and within it I saw shadows that caused fear deep within me, but then the light was turned on within that mansion and I realized that my fear had no substance other than the sound coming as a cry from my own brokenness.

Inside of my dream the lights came on and I began to wander into the rooms of my fear, where nothing was that fearful at all. Within these rooms was plenty and even comfort. I was surprised to see that hell did not reign within my broken heart.

God wants to unveil every secret shadow of your heart. He wants to show you that there is no reality that is greater than His love and peace inside of you. Perfect love casts out fear and love has a way of making us feel safe in our Father's arms. In fact love is the arms of God. When I am in God I am in love. There is no difference between God and love.

Where fear reigns inside of our brokenness we must allow God to turn on the lights and expose the lies within us. The truth sets us free. Many times when

God reveals the truth of our fears we are shocked to discover the unreality and the lack of substance of that fear.

We convinced ourselves that our fears were menacing creatures that lived in our closets when in fact they were just thoughts that bound us. When the lie is exposed the truth does come and then freedom like a rushing wave washes over our hearts.

I pray for you today and ask God to open your heart to his wise counsel. I pray that he will expose the lies that bind you to every fear that has a hold upon your life, including poverty, loneliness, infirmity and lust.

10 PEACE INSIDE THE BOAT

Psalm 4:8
In peace I will lie down and sleep, for you alone, LORD, make me dwell in safety.

There are times that the storm seems to be all around us and that we are being tossed by the waves, but in Christ this is an illusion with no real substance because we will always be alright when Christ is in our boat.

There is no storm that can come against you in Christ that will upset you for long. What we have to do is train ourselves to connect with Holy Spirit when the storm does rise.

There are times when my heart is unnerved by things that seem to arise against me or my family, but I have trained myself to seek the Lord as the first step in overcoming all fears and anxieties, and as a result, I am not destroyed when hardships do come.

Right when the fear is touches my emotions I pray a simple prayer. I say, "Jesus where are you in the midst of this" and then I wait.

His peace then comes like a refreshing wind. It is His peace that I am looking for and that I have trained myself to find. You see God communicates through comfort and peace when hardship arises. When I tap into this peace I tap into the answer to my prayer.

It doesn't matter to me if my circumstances change

right away because as long as I have peace I have freedom in the midst of the storm.

Recently I was boating in the middle of the St. Lawrence Seaway. For those of you not familiar with this piece of God's geography it is absolutely breath taking. I was actually in the thousand island region cruising past many beautiful islands with stunning cottages on each.

Out there in the middle of the bay where giant cargo ships move from the Great Lakes of North America into the Atlantic ocean our little pleasure craft ran out of gas. I was with close friends and my wife and my four young sons. We were stranded and if the weather had turned bad we would have been in a lot of danger.

To complicate things a giant ship began to move toward us. These ships don't get out of your way you must get out of their way. We did not have a paddle on board the boat, but praise God the current moved us out of the shipping lanes and closer to the shore.

In the natural it didn't look good and so I asked God where He was in the middle of all this. His peace came over me. We began to make decisions from the place of His peace and within two hours we were coasting toward our cottage again with gas in our tank.

God's peace will help you to overcome a multitude of problems. As long as you have peace you have everything you need.

You see I figure that if God remains peaceful despite my

circumstances, then I should be peaceful too. The day that God begins to freak out about what I am going through is a day I will truly be worried, but to date he seems to still have peace through all the storms I face, therefore I will be at peace to.

11 PEACE AS THE WAY OF THE SAINT

John 3:16
For God so loved the world that he gave his one and only Son, that whoever believes in him shall not perish but have eternal life.

The way of the Saint is not a principled journey but rather it is a life set on pleasing God. It is not about law, but rather, it is about a freedom that comes from living life in a way that is dictated by heaven itself.

There are many examples of people who have gone before us who determined to have heaven in their hearts no matter what came their way. The light on these people pierced the darkness around them with the light of God. No matter what they faced they continued to exhibit the character of Christ through every trial and storm.

These people were abused and mocked. They faced persecution and some were even beaten and tormented. Some were killed by their enemies and yet continued to reflect Christ to the end. I want to be the same as them, but as long as I live this life I am still on this journey, still being tested.

Many of these people tasted heaven in the most glorious manner. They drank deeply of the spirit of God, became imbued with the light of God, and grew into people who carried his glory and presence.

We are all saints in Christ. We all can reflect His glory.

My heart is to reflect His glory in such a way that the whole world learns that he is God.

I have tasted and seen that the Lord is good and I know that He will be good to everyone who comes into relationship with Him. I also know that life without Him for me was perilous and devoid of any good thing, but in Christ I have experienced such love, peace and joy in my heart. God wants to touch you in the same way.

The way of the Saint is to reflect God's glory to the world around. I don't His glory enough to determine how it should be reflected. I just want Him to have freedom in my life to reflect His goodness in the way that He deems fit.

This might mean that there will be times that reflecting His glory will come in ways very difficult for my mind to understand. It may even be painful for me but He can do what He wants, when He wants and how He wants. I have given Him this permission.

You have to ask yourself, "Are the greatest ambitions in my life for God, or for myself?" We need to pray this often. It is important to understand the motivations of our heart.

It is the battle of every heart. We must lay down self in order to reflect God. There will come many tests from God. You will be put through what feels like fire, but in the end, I believe, that every soul that turns to Christ will find a way to pass that test because God is gracious and kind, and will work with you until you do.

This is the path of grace. It is the way of the saint to reflect God. Once you start on the journey in Christ you become partakers of the same nature that he had on earth. What he was you will be. There are days that this will seems to come easily and then there will be days it will seem that you come kicking and screaming into it, but become a saint you will indeed.

I pray for your minds to be enlightened to the grace and kindness of our God. I pray you will come into a true understanding of grace and not just the artificial intellectual substitute.

12 PEACE UNDER THE BIG TENT

2 Peter 1:2-4
Grace and peace be multiplied to you in the knowledge of God and of Jesus our Lord, as His divine power has given to us all things that pertain to life and godliness, through the knowledge of Him who called us by glory and virtue, by which have been given to us exceedingly great and precious promises, that through these you may be partakers of the divine nature, having escaped the corruption that is in the world through lust.

2 Corinthians 1:20
For all the promises of God in Him are Yes, and in Him Amen, to the glory of God through us...

I have had a number of friends lately write me to tell me that they are going through intense storms in their lives. I understand the storms. They come to all of our lives, but the way through those storms is not to focus on the dark clouds and the thunder and lightning, but rather the way through the storm is to focus on the promises of God for your life.

Recently I was preaching in Lacona, New York for my good friends Sonny and Melody Rudd. They have a tent down on their property and have meetings throughout the summer months. Just as I was about to get up and speak a tornado-like wind came onto the property and the tent started to go up into the air.

For a moment I didn't know what to do - should I stop preaching or should I preach through the storm. People started to run all over the tent reinforcing the supports in case the tent would collapse. One lady ran out into the field where the sun had just set, and where the rains and winds were crashing all around, and began to pray in the spirit for the storm to cease.

I stood in the middle of that tent waiting for wisdom when two friends of mine began to tell me that they thought I should preach through the storm, and so I did.

As I began to speak my mind began to run to the promises of God for my own life. I knew that this storm was not going to take me out because I knew that God had much in store for my life. I began to focus on those promises in the face of the crazy winds, and as one of the main poles began to give way I knew I would not be hurt. There were four salvations that evening.

And that is the way we must be in the face of the dark clouds that rise upon us. We must be bold and hold onto the truth that God has spoken and when the enemy comes with lies and depression and anxiety we must speak in the face of these things and command them to cease.

Just last night I was driving to pick up a friend for supper. On my way a rainbow appeared in the sky and was bursting through a dark cloud. Just above the rainbow an opening appeared in the dark clouds and you could see the fluffy white clouds and blue sky behind them.

I began to hear God say that we are entering a season

of the heavens being opened and the promises of God being poured out. I believe that you also are entering that season and that you should not give up when the darkness comes because God is about to break out over your life. This is His continuous promise to those who love Him.

Just last night my mother had a vision and saw an angel move into her house and all of a sudden people started arriving with many precious gifts for her. I believe that God is saying that he is releasing the angelic hosts on your behalf and that prosperity in every form is about to pour out over all your lives.

The world around us might be in for some dark days, but Christ is rising over the lives of true believers. Many will see the light through our lives in this season because God's blessing will be very pronounced.

13 PEACE OUTSIDE THE BOAT

Matthew 14:29-31

Then Peter got down out of the boat, walked on the water and came toward Jesus. But when he saw the wind, he was afraid and, beginning to sink, cried out, "Lord, save me!"

Immediately Jesus reached out his hand and caught him. "You of little faith," he said, "why did you doubt?"

There are times when it seems that all the odds are piled up against you and to actually step out into something new seems impossible. And yet, inside you can hear the voice of the Lord saying "Get out of the boat."

The safety of the boat can represent our hidden fears of failure. It can represent our social anxieties, our need to be acknowledged or honored. There are many things that can keep us from stepping out of the boat, but it is only when we do step into the unknown that we can become something much different than before.

Can you imagine how Peter must have thought after he walked on water? It must have changed him from the inside out. It must have been exhilarating and he probably had greater faith to believe for greater things.

There have been times that I have stepped out into the unknown having no idea if I was going to sink or swim, and yet because I trusted God, I stepped out anyway and gained a testimony of God's provision or supernatural power. He always comes through when I operate in faith.

It is when I learn to trust God with all my unknowns that I begin to accomplish great things for him. These are the steps of the spirit and each one is like walking on water.

Walking in the spirit for me is walking into the unknown and trusting God to become the rock beneath my feet. I learn to trust Him to keep us me from sinking beneath the wind and the waves. He hasn't let me down yet.

We learn to trust Him in many ways: with our finances, with our health and with our families. We learn to trust Him even when our enemies seem to be surrounding us and gloating over us. We learn to trust Him when our friends turn their backs on us and even when we are all alone.

Have you ever had to step into something brand new? Have you felt the pain of the unknown and succeeded in the face of it. That was the day that you grew into something new and exciting.

God is calling you to step into the new and unknown today. Will you take a giant step for Him and trust Him to become the rock beneath your way. This is the life of faith and the only way to please God. I pray you will be strengthened today.

14 PEACE FROM DAWN TIL DUSK

Proverbs 4:18
The path of the righteous is like the morning sun,
shining ever brighter till the full light of day.

I was attending Bible College in the early 1990's when I was challenged by a story someone told me of Billy Graham, who reportedly read one chapter of Proverbs every day for a season of his life. They further challenged me to do the same thing for one year, and so I did.

Proverbs 4:18 entered my heart in those days. I have always been fascinated with the sunrise. I remember as a teenager in one of my science classes the teacher asked us to get up early to describe the sunrise. I don't know if I ever submitted that report, but I do remember falling in love with God's creation at dawn in that moment. It was the first sunrise I had ever really considered.

Just this morning I was up early to go to work. I went to the gas station to fill up my tank before my 50 kilometer drive downtown.

As I started to pump gas, I glanced up and noticed the sun just piercing the sky in the distance. In the two short minutes that it took me to fill my tank, I watched the sun break the sky and become full circle on the horizon.

This scripture in proverbs came to my mind in that moment. God's word has a way of coming to the surface of our experience when it is planted firmly in our hearts through reading and meditation.

As I have meditated on this scripture in times past I would often think of the breaking of dawn as something negative—as in, my life will be more brilliant come the full light of day, but for now I will have to settle at my light being dimmer.

But as I watched the sun rise this time I looked and saw how much light was in the sky. There was enough to see everything for miles around. The darkness was indeed gone in the coming of the morning light and while the light would increase as the day moved ahead, the morning sun had succeeded in pushing back the darkness.

Even when we are new in Christ, our light shines brightly. Anyone who has watched a rising sun knows the brilliance of that moment—how you have to squint and look away quickly in order to enjoy the break of dawn. You cannot continue to look into it because there would be too much light and pain for your eyes. You glance and then you glance away in order to glance again. You cannot miss the sun rising in that moment. It is there in all its glory.

I just want to encourage you today. Perhaps you feel brand new or perhaps you feel like you lack maturity in Christ. Just know that if you are in Him and He is in you, then His brilliance is in your life. No matter how imperfect you might be, whenever someone in darkness sees you, they squint at the brilliance of your rising life.

15 PEACE OUR HOPE IN CHRIST

Romans 12:12
Be joyful in hope, patient in affliction, faithful in prayer.

When you read this simple scripture closely you begin to see the Christian life within it. The hope of Christ is our very foundation. It was because of what He did on the cross that we have hope at all. In Christ I am a new creation who is no longer bound by the world but now has become a Son of God just like He was a Son of God on earth, and the same peace and joy that was upon Him is now upon me.

The hope that I have is magnificent. Not only do I have a hope for a better life here on earth, but I have an eternity to come where there will be no more suffering, no more sorrow, no more death or mourning or pain (**Revelation 21:4**).

Without Christ there was no hope when the pain came, but now when pain comes I don't focus on it anymore. I know that these old things will pass away and all things will become new (**2 Corinthians 5:17**). In the midst of my sorrow hope arises because I know that what I am suffering is producing a crown of righteousness upon my head. I know that the pain is something from my old nature that is about to die, and that the nature of Christ is taking its place in peace and love.

And when the peace of Christ is in my heart, and afflictions do arise, great strength comes to me because I do not grow weary or impatient. I consider my impatience but then grow past it and instead of becoming angry I grow in longsuffering. Yes, pain, sorrow, depression and anger try to attack me, but with the help of the Holy Spirit I look past these and into the eyes of the King of Peace, who assures me that this too will pass.

Prayer also becomes my greatest weapon against all the pain and lack of knowledge in my life. I pray endlessly for assurance but also for the knowledge to live according to His word. He opens my eyes through prayer and even teaches me to pray His prayers.

There are times that a question comes to my mind for which I do not have an answer, so I assume that this must be a question from the Lord and begin to pray it back to him for the answer. In those moments He opens my eyes to see in ways I never even imagined. Then hope and peace arise.

Before you know it you have walked many miles with Him and look at those who do not believe in wonder. He shows himself so strong to you, and yet, there are those that are faithless all around, that don't believe that God can speak, let alone heal, let alone deliver or let alone bless and favor a life.

And then prayer becomes a weapon against the darkness all around.

You begin to cry out for faith to increase and for those that do not know Him to experience Him. You pray that they will have a vision or a dream that will strengthen them. You pray for them to become everything they were meant to become in Christ. You pray for visitations in people's lives, and then you pray for regions and cities and nations to be touched by the power of God.

And before you know it your hope in Christ has been spread abroad to many hearts and you have prayed for many broken people. They cling to you because of the hope of Christ that is in you. They grip you and shed tears near your feet because you have become a tabernacle, a dwelling place of the Lord Most High. He is always kind, always merciful and gracious to the sinner and when they see His reflection in you they become undone.

16 PEACE THROUGH REVELATION

Hebrews 4:9-11
There remains, then, a Sabbath-rest for the people of God; for anyone who enters God's rest also rests from their works, just as God did from his. Let us, therefore, make every effort to enter that rest, so that no one will perish by following their example of disobedience.

Probably like you I have been told over and over again that I must enter into the rest of God, ceasing from my own labors and only work when God tells me to work.

John 15:5 puts it very eloquently "*I am the vine; you are the branches. If you remain in me and I in you, you will bear much fruit; apart from me you can do nothing.*"

And if you are like me you have prayed and meditated for many years on what it means to actually rest in the Lord.

The other day I had a friend come by my house. She told me that a Man of God gave her a word telling her that she needed to rest from her own labors. This confused her - as it would many of us who receive such a word - because we don't know really know how to rest.

It is not that we don't want to rest, but rather that we have no idea how to rest from our own labors.

The more I live this Christian life the more I have come to believe that in order to rest I need to live by revelation. God needs to speak into my spirit what it means for me to rest every moment of my life. Each moment is different. As each new day presents itself I need revelation for rest for that day. The revelation of rest that I received yesterday is not likely going to do me good today.

What does it mean for me to rest from my labors today? It probably depends on what I find myself laboring for today. Each day I labor for something different. Today I want to sale my house, tomorrow I want to buy a new one. Today I am concerned for my child's welfare, and tomorrow I might be concerned for a loved one who is sick. Perhaps I am worried about money, or my place in ministry, or whether I am being loved, honored or respected.

Each of these can represent hard labor. Each day that I concern myself with a new worry, anxiety or fear I am laboring on my own strength.

The truth is that God has our every day planned out. Jesus taught us to pray for our daily bread, not to worry about tomorrow because tomorrow would worry about itself (**Matthew 6:25-34**).

Resting therefore becomes about laying all our cares on

47

God because we realize that he cares for our every need (**1 Peter 5:7**). Each time a worry comes into our hearts we need to remember His word for our life. When the word is firmly planted in our hearts rest and peace come more easily. Man doesn't live by bread alone but by every word proceeding from God (**Matthew 4:4**).

Recently I was worrying about whether I was making the right decision regarding a particular course in my life. Realizing that much time could be spent worrying about the implications of my decisions I started to pray, fast and seek the Lord about what course I should take.

Through the word of God and through dreams and visions a particular course was laid out before me. As I stepped into it peace came into my heart. It is this "peace" that I call "rest." Every time I am stressed I ask for His revelation and when it comes peace comes.

It doesn't matter how bad your situation is or how deep into trouble you might go because when you get God's revelation on the matter His peace will come.

My favorite scripture is found in **Proverbs 3:5-6**

*Trust in the LORD with all your heart
and lean not on your own understanding;
in all your ways submit to him,
and he will make your paths straight.*

The promise is that as we trust then He will direct. As we trust we learn to rest in the assurance that God is with us. All we have to do is obey when He speaks. This is the hardest part but the reward of obedience is His presence and in His presence there is joy and peace.

So my prayer for you today is that God will teach you to rest in Him for the answers to your problems. May His peace overtake you and may you always have the answer to your problem, and may you have the confidence and trust to obey.

17 PEACE AND GOOD CHEER

There are moments when for no apparent reason my soul feels completely free. I want to write about this while I am feeling it.

Yesterday was a difficult day for me. I felt oppressed on every side and heaviness was like a cap upon my head. I don't want to reflect too long on that feeling because it is not something I want to sense again.

But when the hope of God comes I know that everything is going to be alright. This is like a presence that comes over me and fills me with a spiritual high, a deep contentment or an inner peace. When this occurs there might be no difference between my circumstances from one moment to the next, but my spirit within me is alive in a way that it wasn't a moment before.

Truthfully, I could not live my life without times of refreshing from the Lord. There is no way I could continue in desert places. The desert might be a good place to teach me spiritual lessons, but I long for the refreshing that comes when the Holy Spirit touches my life again.

And certainly, this is the joy of a life lived in Christ - the reward we get for receiving Him into our hearts.

Psalm 30:5 says that *"weeping may last through the night, but joy comes with the morning."* It is this joy that sustains me. It is this joy that feeds me. It is this joy that refreshes me and leads me to higher ground.

Proverbs 17:22 says that *"a cheerful heart is good medicine, but a crushed spirit dries up the bones."*

Joy is more than laughter, although a good laugh is as good as anything to relieve the suffering we may be experiencing. Joy is contentment and hope. Joy is lightness of heart and peace and contentment. When I have joy I have all that I need to get me through my day.

But a crushed heart dries up the bones. Wow! That certainly gives expression to the feeling that we get when we are under oppression. There is this curdling up and rotting that we feel on the inside; a sadness that just does not want to lift. There have been times when I just wish to go and be with the Lord, because certainly that would be better to the dryness that I feel in the moment.

And yet, it isn't death that I am longing for but rather a move of the Holy Spirit in my heart. In those moments when I think absence from the body would be better to the darkness that is surrounding me, I am really really saying that life without the Holy Spirit is death already, and please God come and revive these dry bones again.

So when I feel the joy of the Lord in my heart I am truly thankful. I know that I didn't earn this joy or merit it in anyway, but it was given to me nonetheless. Yes, I might not have earned it but I certainly enjoy it and receive it, just like the dry ground after the rain.

I pray for you today and ask the Lord to give you gladness for your sorrow and a peace that transcends understanding. May you in all your ways shine with the hope of Christ in your inner man. May you walk and not grow weary. Run and not faint.

God bless you all...

ABOUT THE AUTHOR

Darren Canning is a revivalist preacher who travels throughout Canada, the United States and now England. Darren is proud of his circle of friends in ministry. He believes in establishing lifelong relationships with leaders all around the world. From this place of relationship he has seen many regions touched by the power of God. He does conferences on prophetic and healing ministry.

Darren is married to Lydia and has four sons and another child is on the way. He also has two daughters from a previous marriage and one precious grandson.

For more information about Darren Canning go his website www.darrencanning.org

94275269R00035

Made in the USA
Columbia, SC
29 April 2018